WONDERFUL NAMES OF OUR WONDERFUL LORD

Names and Titles
of the Lord Jesus Christ
as Found in the Old and New Testaments

Abridged Edition

Charles E. Hurlburt
and
T. C. Horton

BARBOUR
PUBLISHING

© 2002 by Barbour Publishing, Inc.

ISBN 978-1-58660-737-1

Cover image © PhotoDisc

All Scripture quotations, unless otherwise noted, are taken from the Authorized King James Version of the Bible.

Published by Barbour Publishing, Inc., P.O. Box 719, Uhrichsville, OH 44683, www.barbourbooks.com

Our mission is to publish and distribute inspirational products offering exceptional value and biblical encouragement to the masses.

ecpa Member of the
Evangelical Christian
Publishers Association

Printed in the United States of America.

THE SEED OF THE WOMAN

*"And I will put enmity between thee and the woman,
and between thy seed and her seed."*
Genesis 3:15

B ecause He stooped so low God hath exalted Him very high" (Philippians 2:9, Arthur Way's Translation). From this first great act and fact in His revelation to that last greater act when He died for our sins on Calvary, and up until the very time when God exalted Him very high to sit at His own right hand in the heavenlies, our Savior's example was one of profound humility. He came from the bosom of the Father to become the "SEED OF THE WOMAN." He turned from "the words which I have spoken to you, the same shall judge you," to be in His innocence judged of sinful men and crucified. *Oh, Thou who didst humble Thyself to be born of a woman, who didst bear our sins in Thine own body on the tree, we bow on our faces before Thee and worship and adore. Amen.*

THE ANGEL OF JEHOVAH

*"And the angel of the LORD called unto Abraham
out of heaven the second time."*
Genesis 22:15

T he Angel (or Messenger) of Jehovah was Himself God's message to us. *Oh, Thou who dost Thyself bring Thine own Message to heal our deep desolations— Thou art our sin offering. We praise Thee for the glory which Thou givest in our pain by Thine own radiant presence and worship Thee, Oh "ANGEL OF JEHOVAH." Amen.*

SHILOH (PEACEMAKER)

"The sceptre shall not depart from Judah,
nor a lawgiver from between his feet, until Shiloh come;
and unto him shall the gathering of the people be."
Genesis 49:10

Israel must walk in darkness under law, until the years may seem eternity, but "SHILOH" comes at last and peace. Has SHILOH come to thee? And has the peace which passeth understanding, the peace *He* made entered into thy soul? For Shiloh came and conquered every foe that could harass thee, and stands today offering the peace He made "that passeth knowledge." Hast thou received it? Has SHILOH come in vain for thee? Begin today and "in everything by prayer and supplication make thy requests known to him," and Shiloh's peace shall "keep thy heart."

THE STONE OF ISRAEL

"But his bow abode in strength,
and the arms of his hands were made strong
by the hands of the mighty God of Jacob
(from thence is the shepherd, the stone of Israel)."
Genesis 49:24

Oh "STONE OF ISRAEL," *chief Cornerstone, rejected by the builders, Stone of Stumbling, Rock of Offense, Foundation Stone, on which alone we build aught that shall stand, make me a POLISHED, LIVING stone; built in with other stones; perchance a pillar to go out no more, but always a part of Thy temple, for Thine own in-dwelling. Thrice Holy Lord, self-offered for my peace;*

through death that I might live, through fire that I might become indestructible; consumed that I might feed on Thee in holiest communion—enlighten me today till I perceive Thy peace that passeth understanding. Amen.

Manna

*"And the house of Israel called
the name thereof Manna."*
Exodus 16:31

There is an art, not known to all who travel, by which a wearied and exhausted life may gather, in a way which seems to those who do not understand almost miraculous, new strength, new vigor, new physical power, for an onward march. So does the Master feed the souls of His children Himself a spiritual "Manna" as real and more wonderful than that strange, mysterious food with which He fed the House of Israel. To "feed upon the Lord" may sound like empty mysticism, but may be a fact to every trusting soul. For unto us are given "exceeding great and precious promises, that by him we might be partakers of the divine nature."

The Peace Offering

"And if his oblation be a sacrifice of peace offering. . . he shall offer it without blemish before the LORD."
Leviticus 3:1

Is there any point of dispute between thy Lord and thee? One little thing which thou dost not surrender? He is right. He cannot change. It is *thy* heart which must surrender. Then canst thou receive the peace which passeth knowledge. He has made the offering which atones for all thy past, but thou must yield thy will to Him. Shall it be now?

A STAR

"I shall see him, but not now; I shall behold him,
but not nigh: there shall come a Star out of Jacob,
and a Sceptre shall rise out of Israel,
and shall smite the corners of Moab,
and destroy all the children of Sheth."
Numbers 24:17

What could be more beautiful or more fitting than that our Lord should be called of God "A STAR"? Those who know Him best may say, "I shall see him, but not now. I shall behold him, but not nigh." From far beyond our world of trouble and care and change, He shines with undimmed light, a radiant, guiding STAR to all who follow Him—a morning STAR, promise of a better day.

A SCEPTRE

"A Sceptre shall rise out of Israel."
Numbers 24:17

There is a view of Jesus which men are slow to see, but some day all the world shall know that "A SCEPTRE" shall rise out of Israel, and evil will be destroyed before His righteousness more swiftly than ice must melt before the glowing sun. It is in the very nature of things that sin must be consumed before His glorious holiness. Can it be other than the love of sin that blinds the eyes of men to His consuming righteousness? *"Search me, O God, and know my heart. Try me and know my thoughts, and see if there be any wicked way in me and lead me in the way everlasting."* Amen.

THE MEAT (MEAL) OFFERING

"And when any will offer a meat offering unto the LORD, his offering shall be of fine flour; and he shall pour oil upon it, and put frankincense thereon."
Leviticus 2:1

Perfect communion with our God as shown in the "MEAT OFFERING" was in many senses the highest pattern which our Savior set for men. Shall we not make it the chiefest plan of every day to have a time when we enter into such worship with Him that we may truly say, "There is nothing between Thee and me, dear Lord," and then carry the sweetness of that deep communion unmarred and uninterrupted through all the hours. *Most Holy Meal Offering, El Elyon, as Thou didst pour upon the fine meal of Thy perfect life the Holy Oil of Thy most Holy Spirit, and the frankincense of Thy perfect adoration, and offer all for me, so I, accepting Thine which only hallows mine, pour forth my soul, my blood-cleansed soul, in worship. Holy! Holy! Holy! is the Lord. Amen.*

THE ROCK OF MY SALVATION

"The LORD liveth; and blessed be my rock; and exalted be the God of the rock of my salvation."
2 Samuel 22:47

No graver danger threatens the believer than that of forgetting that he was redeemed—forgetting even in the joy of realized life what our salvation cost, and what is the rock foundation of our faith. To meet this need our Savior pictures Himself not merely as the Rock of Ages, and our Strong Rock of Refuge, but the *Rock of our Salvation.* Here, in Him and upon His merit and atoning grace, we were saved from among the lost. Let us glory in this precious name and never forget that He was "wounded for our transgressions" and "that he bore our sins in his own body on the tree."

THE LIGHT OF THE MORNING

"And he shall be as the light of the morning, when the sun riseth, even a morning without clouds."
2 Samuel 23:4

No single name nor picture of our Lord could possibly reveal Him as the full supply of all our need. Our Lord is to His people not only "The Morning Star" but when the lights of night shall fade in dawning day, He becomes the "LIGHT OF THE MORNING." When all of earth has passed, when all earth's visions fade and flee away, when the great glory of that morning of our eternal life in Heaven shall break upon us, we shall find that He who lighted all our earthly pilgrimage is still our source of life and guidance over there, and will be to those for whom He has prepared a place, the "LIGHT OF THE MORNING." "So shall we be forever with the Lord."

THE CAPTAIN OF THE HOST OF THE LORD

"And he said, Nay; but as captain of the host of the LORD am I now come."
Joshua 5:14

The hosts of Israel stand before the gateway to a promised land. No swords are drawn, no skill have they, but with them is an unseen host, and with the host, "THE CAPTAIN OF JEHOVAH'S HOST." Jericho and all the giants of the land submit, and for thee, "behind the dim unknown standeth God within the shadows, keeping watch above His own."

Captain of the Hosts of God,
In the path where Thou hast trod,
Bows my soul in humble awe—
Take command. Thy word is law.

Cause me to possess the land,
Led by Thine Almighty hand.
Be my guide, defense and power,
Lead me from this very hour. Amen.

TENDER GRASS

*"And he shall be. . .as the tender grass springing out of
the earth by clear shining after rain."*
2 Samuel 23:4

Sheep thrive best in pastures so low and short that
other animals are not able to eat it. The good
Shepherd leads His flock in pastures where the "tender
grass," springing up from the earth after the rain, brings
to them all-sufficient nourishment as they feed on Him.
Oh, ye who are partakers of the Divine nature, open now
the Book of books, and humbly kneeling feed on Him
who is the Living Word, "THE TENDER GRASS," which sat-
isfies and builds up His hungry sheep.

THE DAYSMAN

*"Neither is there any daysman betwixt us,
that might lay his hand upon us both."*
Job 9:33

When the day of reckoning comes, when by all justice I should hear the sentence which my sins
deserve, when I shall stand before the Father, stripped of
all pretense and shame, then will I fear no evil, for my
"DAYSMAN," Mediator, Arbitrator, will stand and speak
for me. Can I do less than bow upon my face and worship
Him, now, and throughout eternity?

My Glory

*"But thou, O LORD, art a shield for me;
my glory, and the lifter up of mine head."*
Psalm 3:3

That God is "glory"—or "excellence"—beyond our understanding, none can deny. But do our hearts look up to Him today in humble, earnest worship, and know the truth, and speak the truth—"Thou art MY GLORY"? Our *safety* lies in the fact that He possesses us. Our deepest, holiest *joy* comes only when we humbly say in the hour of secret worship, "Thou art mine." *Oh, Lord my Glory, be Thou my shield this day. Amen.*

The Lifter Up of Mine Head

*"But thou, O LORD, art a shield for me;
my glory, and the lifter up of mine head."*
Psalm 3:3

Oh, Thou who hast given
    Thy glory to me,
Anoint my blind eyes
    Till Thy glory I see.

Lift up my bowed head,
    Be my shield and my light,
Till Thy radiant glory
    Shall banish my night.

FORTRESS

"The LORD is my rock and my fortress,
and my deliverer; my God, my strength,
in whom I will trust; my buckler,
and the horn of my salvation, and my high tower."
Psalm 18:2

A mighty fortress is my God," and no evil may reach the soul that shelters there. There is no saint of God who may look back through all the troubled years of any earthly pilgrimage, and not say, if he shall truly speak, "I have been kept by the power of God." Every failure of our lives and each defeat has come when we have sought some earthly fortress rather than our Lord. *I am hiding, Lord, in Thee. Amen.*

MY ROCK AND MY FORTRESS

"For thou art my rock and my fortress;
therefore for thy name's sake lead me, and guide me."
Psalm 31:3

S ome day our work shall all be tried by storm and by fire and the question will be of our foundation. Are we built upon the Rock of Ages, that High Rock which is a Fortress, so that, though the wind blows and the storm shakes all about us, we shall stand secure? And if Christ be our "ROCK" and our "FORTRESS" shall we build with "wood and hay and stubble" upon such an eternal foundation? *Lord Jesus, may we seek to gather "gold and silver and precious stones," that we may bring some honor to Thee, our "ROCK AND FORTRESS," by building that which shall endure through all the ages. Amen.*

RESTORER

*"He restoreth my soul; he leadeth me in the paths
of righteousness for his name's sake."*
Psalm 23:3

We wander from God and from the paths of righteousness—from following Him beside the still waters—till we lose the way, lose joy, lose the sound of His voice. Then the Master "restoreth (the only use of this form in the Old Testament) our soul"; "brings us back into His way," into the paths of righteousness. *Oh, gracious "RESTORER," bring back my wandering soul as a straying sheep, and lead me on in the paths of righteousness "for Thy name's sake." Amen.*

A WORM AND NO MAN

*"But I am a worm, and no man; a reproach of men,
and despised of the people."*
Psalm 22:6

Few harder experiences come to God's children than in these days when those who should be friendly, unjustly make us a reproach, and when they say in the midst of trials which are not the result of any sin in us, "Aha, Aha," as though they themselves are righteous, when perchance their sin has brought to us the pain—yet *He* has walked that way before us. He too was "A Reproach of Men"! Shall not the servant walk there too, and be like Him who in such suffering "opened not His mouth"? *Lord Jesus, who did'st bear scorn and reproach for me, give me the grace of true humility. Amen.*

MY SHEPHERD

"The LORD is my shepherd; I shall not want."
Psalm 23:1

To say, "The Lord is MY SHEPHERD," must carry with it in our understanding not merely grateful praise for the infinite grace and tenderness of the Great Shepherd who leads us by still waters and in green pastures, but confession of our own helplessness and need of a Shepherd's care. And a remembrance also of our lost, undone condition, until

> "All through the mountains, thunder-riven,
> And up from the rocky steep,
> There arose a glad cry to the gates of heaven,
> 'Rejoice! I have found My sheep!' "

Lord Jesus, Thou tender Shepherd, lead us forth this day in glad service for Thee. Amen.

THE STRONG AND MIGHTY JEHOVAH

"Who is the King of glory? Jehovah, strong and mighty, Jehovah mighty in battle."
Psalm 24:8 RV

Is thy heart faint? Thy strength but utter weakness? Behold thy LORD—Jehovah—"He who reveals Himself" as "STRONG AND MIGHTY"—a soldier, a warrior, with sufficient power to break down every opposition. Hear Him say, "My presence shall go with thee to conquer every foe." *Strong and mighty Jehovah, give me victory over all the power of the enemy this day. Amen.*

JEHOVAH, MIGHTY IN BATTLE

"Who is the King of glory?. . .
Jehovah, mighty in battle."
Psalm 24:8 RV

No life can be lived for God in these difficult days without terrific conflict. Foes within and foes without assail each saint continuously. Principalities and powers are arrayed against the child of God who seeks to serve his Master. We have no might with which to meet "this great host that cometh out against us," but JEHOVAH, MIGHTY IN BATTLE, is our Savior, our Intercessor, our Elder Brother, our ever-present Friend. *"Sure, I must fight if I would win; increase my courage, Lord."* Amen.

A STRONG TOWER

"For thou hast been a shelter for me,
and a strong tower from the enemy."
Psalm 61:3

What is the testimony of our souls today as we read that which others have said concerning Him who has been a "STRONG TOWER" from the enemy? Did ever a child of God in danger hasten within the Strong Tower of His Presence and find aught of failure or defeat? Must we not confess that every failure has come when we were found outside? *Oh, Thou Strong Tower, may we enter in today and dwell in Thee and be safe.*

KING OF GLORY

"Who is this King of glory?
The LORD of hosts, he is the King of glory."
Psalm 24:10

Jehovah Jesus, the glorious King! Not merely a king, but glorious, excelling all others in mighty truth and power, grace and love. We almost forget for a time His absolute sovereignty as we bow in humble worship before His matchless glory, and cry again and again, *"Thy Kingdom come,"* Oh, Glorious King. Amen.

MY STRONG ROCK

"Bow down thine ear to me; deliver me speedily;
be thou my strong rock, for an house
of defense to save me."
Psalm 31:2

No sorrow of men is so deep and dark and bitter as to be without refuge, a rock, a safe retreat. My soul, however deep thy sorrow, however dark thy sin, however hopeless thy lot among men, the Man of Sorrows bore thy sin in His own body on the tree. He carried all thy grief. He is thy "STRONG ROCK." A strong, safe house, in which I am defended from myself, the world, the devil.

"Rock of ages, cleft for me,
Let me hide myself in Thee."
Amen.

WISDOM

*"I wisdom dwell with prudence,
and find out knowledge of witty inventions."*
Proverbs 8:12

Wisdom is the right use of knowledge. What a wondrous name for Him who gave Himself for us! Who, "when He putteth forth His own sheep goeth before them"; who guides us by the skillfulness of His hand. *May we seek with all our hearts until we find Thee, and finding Thee, find* WISDOM *to do the will of God. Amen.*

THE KING'S SON

*"Give the king thy judgment, O God,
and thy righteousness unto the king's son."*
Psalm 72:1

How little do our hearts discern the homage due to God as KING and to Jesus as His SON. We bow our heads, we lift our hats, we pay our homage to the fleeting, trifling power of earth's great men, but do we, as we enter the house of God, bow humbly and revere "THE KING'S SON?" Are earthly thoughts hushed and earthly words stilled as we gather in the house of God, and even when our spokesman voices our desires to Him, do wandering thoughts of earthly things deprive us of the blessing and the answer to our prayers? *Lord, teach us how to pray, that we may truly worship Thee. Amen.*

A Stranger and an Alien

"I am become a stranger unto my brethren,
and an alien unto my mother's children."
Psalm 69:8

What was the price He paid,
    That, what He bore for me;
"A Stranger, an Alien"; alone,
    He died on Calvary.

A "Stranger" to make me a friend,
    An "Alien" to give me a home.
Great Stranger, I fall at Thy feet,
    No longer from Thee will I roam.
                Amen.

Rain Upon Mown Grass

"He shall come down like rain upon the mown grass."
Psalm 72:6

My soul was parched with the fire of sin,
    My life mowed down with pain,
My Saviour spoke, "My child, draw near."
    His word was like the Rain.

Refreshing, cleansing, lifting me,
    My Lord, My All, came down,
And now I turn from all earth's dross—
    To gain a Heavenly crown.

My First-Born

*"Also I will make him my first-born,
higher than the kings of the earth."*
Psalm 89:27

L oose thy shoes from off thy feet, for the place where thou standest is holy." The Eternal Father, God is speaking. "My First-born I will make higher than the kings of earth." Oh, thou who art the last-born of the Father, the First-born is thy Elder Brother. Thou hast shared His humiliation to thy salvation. Thou shalt share His exaltation to thine eternal glory. *We worship Thee; Lord Jesus, God's "First Born"! Amen.*

My High Tower

*"My goodness, and my fortress; my high tower,
and my deliverer; my shield, and he in whom I trust;
who subdueth my people under me."*
Psalm 144:2

M y High Tower" is a vision of our glorious Savior as the Most High—high above our trials; high above our temptations; high above our foes; high above our failures and losses; high above the fret and care of our earthward life. A place of holy calm and peace and stillness. The door is open. *Lord Jesus, our High Tower, let us enter in today. Amen.*

THE ROSE OF SHARON

"I am the rose of Sharon."
Song of Solomon 2:1

Child of God, there is no mood of thy life where Jesus fails to fit thy need; to brighten as a brilliant rose thy life. In joy or sorrow, sunshine or shadow, day or night, He blooms for thee. Behold Him, then, today, not only on the Cross for thee, not only on the Throne, but near thee, close beside thy path, "THE ROSE OF SHARON."

THE ROCK THAT IS HIGHER THAN I

"From the end of the earth will I cry unto thee,
when my heart is overwhelmed;
lead me to the rock that is higher than I."
Psalm 61:2

Not down to a dungeon deep,
    Nor to level of earth, hard by—
But lead, when the storm o'erwhelms,
    To "THE ROCK THAT IS HIGHER THAN I."

Up from my sin's dark slime,
    Away from the world's mad cry—
To Thee do I come, O Christ!
    To "THE ROCK THAT IS HIGHER THAN I."

There will I worship and wait
    Redeemed, with the saints on high.
All glory, and honor, and praise
    To "THE ROCK THAT IS HIGHER THAN I."

EXCELLENT

*"Let them praise the name of the LORD;
for his name alone is excellent."*
Psalm 148:13

A ll the glory of the Lord is that in which He excels all others." "His name is EXCELLENT," and all His names which represent some feature of His grace are glorious because they excel any other name ever uttered among men. What friend, what helper do we know on earth that ever has or can approach His excellence? And so we turn with new deep joy to the Psalmist's testimony, "They that know thy name shall put their trust in thee."

SHOWERS UPON THE EARTH

*"He shall come down like rain upon the mown grass,
as showers that water the earth."*
Psalm 72:6

O ur lives grow dusty, dry, and desert in our earthly pilgrimage, but He who seeks a love that is fresh and pure and strong comes down upon us as "THE SHOWERS UPON THE EARTH." Have you turned to Him today and found that cool, refreshing, cleansing blessing which He seeks to give?

*"There shall be showers of blessing,
Oh, that today they might fall!
Now, as to God we're confessing,
Now, as on Jesus we call."*

Amen

UNDERSTANDING

"Counsel is mine, and sound wisdom;
I am understanding; I have strength."
Proverbs 8:14

God is Love, God is Light, God is to us a thousand things for which we long and which we need, but have we realized that in possessing Him and abiding in Him, He is "UNDERSTANDING" and all that seems dark and difficult will become clear to us as we depend upon Him, who is "UNDERSTANDING"? It would take ten thousand years to learn a few of the many things we long to know on earth. The soul that is linked to God begins to understand and will go on to clearer understanding throughout the countless ages.

THE HEAD STONE OF THE CORNER

"The stone which the builders refused is
become the head stone of the corner."
Psalm 118:22

Men may reject "THE HEAD STONE OF THE CORNER" and seek to erect a building that shall stand, without the Living Christ. But God has laid aside all human plans and made our Lord and Savior "THE HEAD STONE OF THE CORNER." When all human buildings crumble and every man-taught architect has failed, all hearts bow before that perfect building, that eternal temple, worshiping Him who is its crown of grace.

A Friend That Sticketh Closer Than a Brother

*"A man that hath friends must shew himself friendly;
and there is a friend that
sticketh closer than a brother."*
Proverbs 18:24

Stay, lonely pilgrim, searching long for fellowship. Stop here and find "A Friend." "There is a Friend," though all the world deny it. One who is always true and faithful. One who never leaves and ne'er forsakes. No brother will, or can, abide as He. Will you be friend to Jesus, as He is friend to thee? *We worship Thee, we trust all to Thee, and take from Thee all peace, all grace, all needed power to do and be what pleaseth Thee, our never-absent Friend. Amen.*

Ointment Poured Forth

*"Because of the savour of thy good ointments
thy name is as ointment poured forth."*
Song of Solomon 1:3

Is thy soul sore from sin, from chafing, or from the fiery darts of Satan, of sinners, or of saints? Then is thy Lord to thee as "Ointment Poured Forth," free, abundant, ready, healing and fragrant. Suffering soul, come near to Him and let that healing Ointment pour over thee and soothe and heal thee.

A BUNDLE OF MYRRH

"A bundle of myrrh is my well beloved unto me."
Song of Solomon 1:13

O h, Child of Sorrow, Church of Smyrna, sad soul suffocating in earth's dark vapors, thy Lord is for thee an exquisite perfume, "A BUNDLE OF MYRRH." A missionary, wearily walking a winding pathway in the night, suddenly came upon a spot where the air was heavy with the perfume of wild jasmine, and was comforted and refreshed by a fragrance preserved from nonappreciative wild animals and wilder men for a sorrowing toiler. So is thy Lord, to thee, "A BUNDLE OF MYRRH."

A CLUSTER OF CAMPHIRE

"My beloved is unto me as a cluster of camphire
in the vineyard of En-gedi."
Song of Solomon 1:14

A beautiful, fragrant flower—"a cluster" of them— exquisite beauty, exquisite perfume in abundance! Struggling in the midst of experiences that are not fragrant, that are not delightful, hast thou learned to turn to Him, who, in the midst of darkness, is Light, in the midst of battle, is Peace, in the midst of unpleasantness, is to thee unlimited and exquisite delight? Dost thou know thy Lord as "A CLUSTER OF CAMPHIRE"? Acquaint now thyself with Him, and be at peace.

THE LILY OF THE VALLEYS

"I am. . .the lily of the valleys."
Song of Solomon 2:1

S weetest, fairest, most exquisite flower that eye hath
seen hidden save to eyes that seek it out. So does Thy
Lord unveil Himself to thee, even though thou walkest
through the valleys. Only in those deeper shadows canst
thou know His utter loveliness. Behold *Him* then, and
"fear no evil."

HIM WHOM MY SOUL LOVETH

"I will rise now and go about the city in the streets,
and in the broad ways I will seek
him whom my soul loveth."
Song of Solomon 3:2

Not in the doubting throng,
    Not in the boastful song,
But kneeling—with Christ above me—
    Humbly I'll say, "I love Thee."

Not with my lips alone,
    Not for Thy gifts I own,
But just for the grace I see
    Jesus, my soul loveth Thee. *Amen.*

THE CHIEFEST AMONG
TEN THOUSAND

"My beloved is white and ruddy,
the chiefest among ten thousand."
Song of Solomon 5:10

Do we sometimes sing with too little depth of meaning, "He's the chiefest of ten thousand to my soul"? Is He really first in our hearts' affection? If so, His presence has been real to us for He has said, "Ye shall seek me and ye shall find me, when ye search for me with all your heart," or, "with your whole desire." Here the secret of full transforming communion with our Lord Jesus Christ is found in gazing upon Him in all the beauty of His holiness, until in very truth He becomes in our hearts the "CHIEFEST AMONG TEN THOUSAND."

THE CHILD

"For before the child shall know to refuse the evil,
and choose the good, the land that thou abhorrest
shall be forsaken of both her kings."
Isaiah 7:16

The first, last and chiefest mark of Christ's Deity was His great humility. The greatest Sage and Seer of all the ages, "A CHILD"! The Everlasting God, hoary-white with eternal years, "A CHILD"! Then shall *we* hesitate to "become as little children" knowing that only so shall we enter the kingdom?

THE BRANCH OF THE LORD

"In that day shall the branch of the LORD
be beautiful and glorious."
Isaiah 4:2

By every means and picture which we can understand the Spirit reveals our Savior's oneness with God. None is more clear or full of meaning to us than this, "THE BRANCH OF THE LORD." One with the Father, growing out of and yet a part of Him. And we are "branches" of Christ (see John 15). As we worship the Christ who is very God, we hear Him say, "If ye abide in me, ye shall ask what ye will, and it shall be done unto you."

ALTOGETHER LOVELY

"His mouth is most sweet;
yea, he is altogether lovely."
Song of Solomon 5:16

Every earthly joy will pall,
    Every earthly friend will fall.
Only Christ is to the end
    "ALTOGETHER LOVELY," Friend.

Do you see His wondrous face?
    Full of glory, love and grace?
Look, and all thy need confess,
    Worship His pure Holiness.

JEHOVAH OF HOSTS

"And one cried unto another, and said,
Holy, holy, holy is Jehovah of hosts:
the whole earth is full of his glory."
Isaiah 6:3

The "Jehovah" of the Old Testament is the "Jesus" of the New. If we always think (as Scofield suggested) of Jehovah as "God revealing Himself," and the words of Jehovah-Jesus, "Blessed are the pure in heart for they shall see God," then shall the heavens about us be always full of the chariots and horsemen of JEHOVAH OF HOSTS, and all fear shall be stilled and His revelation of Himself to us will not be in vain. *Lord Jesus, Jehovah of hosts, give us a vision of Thy glory this day. Amen.*

A SANCTUARY

"And he shall be for a sanctuary."
Isaiah 8:14

Where is thy place of worship? Where, in the turmoil of the street; where, in the busy cares of home; where, in the hurry and confusion of men, shall our souls find the place to pray? "He shall be for a 'SANCTUARY,' closer to thee than breathing, nearer than hands or feet." At any moment during all the hurried day thou mayest be hidden from all earth's eyes, and still from all earth's din. Only abide in Him.

A GREAT LIGHT

"The people that walked in darkness
have seen a great light;
they that dwell in the land of the shadow of death,
upon them hath the light shined."
Isaiah 9:2

It is the people who once walked in darkness who are able to see the greatness of the light. It is the soul which finds that it is lost that seeks the Lord. Have *you* seen the LIGHT? The beloved apostle said, "That which we have seen, declare we unto you, and this is the message that we declare unto you that God is Light, and in Him is no darkness." *Lord, let my life and lips tell out the story of the LIGHT my eyes have seen. Amen.*

THE EVERLASTING FATHER

"For unto us a child is born,
unto us a son is given. . .
and his name shall be called. . .
The everlasting Father."
Isaiah 9:6

Who has not mourned a father's death and felt the loss of his transient power and helpfulness? The child who was born in Bethlehem, who gave His life for thee, is not alone thy Savior and thy King, but "His name shall be called THE EVERLASTING FATHER." In His everlasting love, within His everlasting arms, within His Father-heart which pitieth thee—His child, thou shalt find safety, rest and comfort.

COUNSELLOR

"For unto us a child is born,
unto us a son is given. . .
and his name shall be called. . .Counsellor."
Isaiah 9:6

Not often is He called "COUNSELLOR" now. Even God's saints continuously ask of men instead of God, "How may I find God's will?" Conference after conference is held by both the world and the church to find by human wisdom some better plan for earthly government, or for the church, or for the welfare of our earthly life and walk. But how rarely do we bow together or alone to seek that Heavenly wisdom, that Divine counsel, which alone will enable us to find our way out of the mazes in which we wander. When shall His Name be joyfully and triumphantly proclaimed as "Counsellor" by His people? By thee?

THE MIGHTY GOD

"For unto us a child is born,
unto us a son is given. . .
and his name shall be called. . .
The mighty God."
Isaiah 9:6

Have we doubted His might and feared, in the day when some foe was near? Hark! His name is "THE MIGHTY GOD." Then away with all doubt and fear! "Thou hast made both the heaven and earth. There is nothing too hard for Thee." *Lord, I bow to the dust and worship. Mighty God, show Thy power in me! Amen.*

WONDERFUL

"For unto us a child is born, unto us a son is given. . .
his name shall be called. . .Wonderful."
Isaiah 9:6

JESUS is "the same yesterday, today, and forever," and men who think Him commonplace or at most only an unusual man, will some-time stand ashamed and confounded as they hear this prophecy fulfilled, "His name shall be called WONDERFUL." Today He is working just as wonderful works as when He created the heaven and the earth. His wondrous grace, His wonderful omnipotence, is for His child who needs Him and who trusts Him, even today. Attempt great things for God and expect great things from Him and you will begin even now to say, His name is WONDERFUL.

THE PRINCE OF PEACE

"For unto us a child is born, unto us a son is given. . .
and his name shall be called. . .The Prince of Peace."
Isaiah 9:6

He who proclaimed to loyal hearts, "My peace I leave with you. My peace I give unto you. Not as the world giveth give I unto you," is rightly called "THE PRINCE OF PEACE." He who brought such peace to earth was rejected of men, and waits still to be crowned on earth; but He gives before that royal day a peace that passeth understanding to every trusting heart. Have you received it? Will you, in loyalty to "THE PRINCE OF PEACE," accept in humble faith His peace today?

THE LIGHT OF ISRAEL

*"And the light of Israel shall be for a fire, and his Holy
One for a flame; and it shall burn and devour his
thorns and his briers in one day."*
Isaiah 10:17

JESUS was and is the "LIGHT OF ISRAEL." He is also the
"Light of life" and the "Light of men," a "Light to
lighten the world." But the "Light of Israel" was "to burn
and devour thorns and briers." Dear child of God, are you
bringing the useless branches, the unpleasant, unlovely
things of your life into the Light of His Presence that they
may be consumed? Some day the shining of His Presence
will destroy the very Advocate of evil. Shall we not submit our lives to that Wondrous Light and ask Him to con-
sume all evil in us?

A ROD OUT OF THE STEM OF JESSE

*"And there shall come forth a rod out of the stem of
Jesse, and a Branch shall grow out of his roots."*
Isaiah 11:1

ONLY a "rod" from a human "stem"? Only a "root"
from "dry ground"? Hath He no "form nor comeliness," no "beauty that we should desire"? "Surely He
bore our griefs" and the way of "our peace" was in Him.
"Because He stooped so low God hath exalted Him very
high," and the comeliness of a tender plant was the glory
of God on high.

A BRANCH OUT OF HIS ROOTS

"And. . .a Branch shall grow out of his roots."
Isaiah 11:1

Of all the miracles that attest to the Deity of our Lord, including the miraculous preservation of the Scriptures, none is more wonderful or convincing to the honest, faithful heart than the preservation, not only of Israel, but of that section of Israel, humble in its origin, which revealed our Lord to be born of the family of David and of Jesse. Out of the nations scattered over the earth, out of the line of kings who long had ceased to reign, there came forth, as the prophet said, a "BRANCH OUT OF HIS ROOTS" of the stem of Jesse. And He who was of the seed of David shall just as surely come again to reign once more over Israel, and through Israel over all the earth. *Lord, our faint hearts believe anew in God's eternal truth and faithfulness. Amen.*

THE ROOT OF JESSE

*"And in that day there shall be a root of Jesse. . .
to it shall the Gentiles seek;
and his rest shall be glorious."*
Isaiah 11:10

It is not Israel alone who shall rejoice when "a root of Jesse shall stand for an ensign of the people," for "to it shall the Gentiles seek," and all the gracious promises and gifts God gave to Jesse and to David and his seed which could bring rest and comfort to our souls belong to us who worship Jesus, David's Son, and Jesse's Root. How all the grace and glory of our God through all the ages, is gathered up for us who from the Gentile world bow at His feet and find glorious rest!

My Strength and My Song

"Behold, God is my salvation;
I will trust, and not be afraid:
for the LORD JEHOVAH is my strength and my song;
he also is become my salvation."
Isaiah 12:2

We know Jehovah is our "STRENGTH" but do we make Him also our "SONG"? As we make Him so and sing of Him, we lose our fear. We are able to "trust and not be afraid," only as we *sing* of Him. Our Redeemer is our "STRENGTH." Make Him your "SONG" today.

The Ensign of the People

"And in that day there shall be a root of Jesse,
which shall stand for an ensign of the people;
to it shall the Gentiles seek;
and his rest shall be glorious."
Isaiah 11:10

Jesus is the people's flag, an "ENSIGN OF THE PEOPLE." Wherever and whenever He is lifted up the people seek after Him. Is not our failure to win many to the Lord due to our misrepresentation of Him? To our failure to reveal the beauty of His holiness and to enter into His glorious rest? Shall we bow in humble confession while we pray that we who are His representatives may be saved from misrepresentation of Him by lives that are cruelly unlike Him and seek for grace to exalt Him everywhere among men?

A Nail Fastened
in a Sure Place

*"And I will fasten him as a nail
in a sure place and he shall be for
a glorious throne to his father's house."*
Isaiah 22:23

Men have dreamed fantastic ideas concerning Christ as a "NAIL IN A SURE PLACE." Whatever else this name may or may not mean, it brings to the worshiping child of God a sense of the fixedness, the certainty and security of Jesus Christ in His relationship to the temple and throne of God. If we on earth are being builded together for an habitation of God, yet more sure is the fact of the presence of Christ filling the house. If we are "pillars who go no more out," it is because He is secure—His place is "fastened" and "sure." "So shall we be ever with the Lord," for where He is, there shall also His servant be, and our abiding is as sure as Christ's.

A Glorious Throne to His
Father's House

*"And he shall be for a glorious throne to
his father's house."*
Isaiah 22:23

One of the most vivid pictures painted by the Holy Spirit of the life that lies beyond follows in the Revelation—the swift, wondrous vision of the church on earth (Revelation 4:2-3). "Behold a throne was set in heaven. . . and there was a rainbow round about the throne." That rainbow brings us hope and comfort and the precious, glorious promise that our Lord Himself is a "Glorious Throne to His Father's House." Let it be no longer hard or difficult for thee to pray. The throne before which you bow is not one of austere justice but rather one of infinite grace. Let us therefore come boldly to the Throne of Grace, that we may obtain mercy and find help.

The Rock of Ages

"Trust ye in Jehovah forever; for in Jehovah,
even Jehovah, is an everlasting rock."
(Margin, "rock of ages.")
Isaiah 26:4

Many of the college buildings at Oxford University, hundreds of years old, were described by one who studied there more than half a century ago as "leprous with age." Many are crumbling away, and some must be replaced to save the buildings. The strongest rocks in which men hide the bodies of departed friends are ofttimes riven by a growing plant. But He who calls us to "trust in Jehovah forever" calls Himself *"An Everlasting Rock"* or "The Rock of Ages." Let us trust in Him today, tomorrow, and forever.

STRENGTH TO THE POOR
AND NEEDY

"For thou has been a strength to the poor,
a strength to the needy in his distress."
Isaiah 25:4

Touched with the feeling of our infirmities our Lord in His omnipotence becomes a "STRENGTH TO THE POOR AND NEEDY." Let us never forget that His strength is made perfect in our weakness only when we realize our helplessness and fling ourselves, as trusting children, into the outstretched arms by which He "created the heavens and the earth." With what wondrous picture does our Lord reveal Himself as the supply for our every need and "strength to the poor"!

A CROWN OF GLORY

"In that day shall the Lord of hosts be for a crown
of glory. . .unto the residue of his people."
Isaiah 28:5

We hear and think much of redeemed and fruitful saints shining as stars in the diadem of our Lord, but in this wondrous title of our glorious Savior we have a new vision of His relationship to His people. Souls who have been down-trodden and scorned by those whom the world calls great, will in that day as He honors redeemed believers as His Bride, find that the presence, the tender and gracious love of the King of Glory, will be to them in the eyes of all, a witness, a "CROWN OF GLORY." Oh, thou who art redeemed from among the lost, thou who wast dead and art alive, wast lost and art found, behold His wondrous grace! The King of kings, the Lord of lords, shall be to thee a CROWN OF GLORY. Then fall at His feet today and worship Him with all thy heart.

A SHADOW FROM THE HEAT

"For thou hast been. . .a shadow from the heat."
Isaiah 25:4

In the intolerable heat of the sun as it beats upon plateaus of equatorial Africa, one may step from the unbearable heat to a shade so cool, so refreshing, that until it is experienced it is almost beyond conception or belief. Thus our Lord pictures Himself to His weary, toiling children, struggling onward in the heat of almost impossible experiences, as a "SHADOW FROM THE HEAT," into whose presence we may step at any moment of our pilgrimage, and find cool, refreshing rest.

A DIADEM OF BEAUTY

"In that day shall the Lord of hosts be for. . .a diadem of beauty, unto the residue of his people."
Isaiah 28:5

The difference between a Crown of Glory and a "DIADEM OF BEAUTY" is that in the first the excellence, the worth, the value, the glory of God shall be upon the saints. While in the other, the beauty, the very radiance of the Lord, shall fill and shine out from those who, in a moment, in the twinkling of an eye, shall be changed into His likeness. O, humble child of God, behold the exceeding grace which shall be revealed in the ages to come. The beauty of the Lord our God shall be upon thee, and He shall be to thee a crown or DIADEM OF BEAUTY. "He that hath this hope in him purifieth himself."

THE FOUNDATION

"Therefore thus saith the Lord God, Behold,
I lay in Zion for a foundation a stone."
Isaiah 28:16

Of all the gracious promises concerning the children of God none is more wonderful than that which describes the saints as polished stones in the temple where He dwells. With Divine grace our Lord calls Himself "THE FOUNDATION," an "Everlasting Rock," "The Rock of Ages." Where stands our faith today? Are we building upon the sands of human philosophies, or upon Him?

"On the Rock of Ages founded,
Naught can shake our sure repose."

A SURE FOUNDATION

"Therefore thus saith the Lord God, Behold,
I lay in Zion. . .a sure foundation."
Isaiah 28:16

All the chiseling, all the polishing of experiences through which we pass, is costly. Will it last? Is it worth while? Worth while to suffer on and say, "Dear Lord, stay not thine hand to comfort us and steady us." Through just such testing times the Master calls Himself a "SURE FOUNDATION." No experiment here, no doubt, no room for anxious thought or fear. He who builds upon the "SURE FOUNDATION" finds his building sure, and he shall be a "pillar in the temple of God," to "go no more out forever."

AN HIDING PLACE
FROM THE WIND

*"And a man shall be as
an hiding place from the wind."*
Isaiah 32:2

Standing one day on the deck of a steamer in the harbor at Aden, a traveler saw a storm of wind sweeping across the desert like some high, mountainous wave, rolling and sweeping forward until it struck the ships lying there at anchor, till nearly every boat was torn from it moorings or forced to loosen every cable and steam with full force into the face of the terrific wind. No hiding place was there. So do the storms of hate, of evil, and of sin sweep over our lives as we journey toward our everlasting home. But for every soul who knows his own helplessness, our Savior is Himself "AN HIDING PLACE FROM THE WIND."

A TRIED STONE

"Therefore thus saith the Lord God, Behold,
I lay in Zion a foundation, a stone,
a tried stone, a precious corner stone."
Isaiah 28:16

How strange is this experience of our Lord. Surely the Father knew the Son, knew His every capacity and power. Yet He was tried of God as we have need to be tried, only that He might leave us an "example that we might walk in His steps." What mockery, what hopeless blasphemy, that He should be rejected by some builders! Let us bid the great Master Builder to try us and to chisel us until we fit in the place which He has prepared for us.

A COVERT FROM THE TEMPEST

"And a man shall be as a. . .
covert from the tempest."
Isaiah 32:2

Of no other being could such language be used, in no other literature of the world is such marvelous imagery to be found, as that used in the Word of God to picture the grace and glory of our Lord. When the destructive tempests sweep and we hide in Him, shall we be safe? He shall be a "COVERT FROM THE TEMPEST"—covered, sheltered, safe. Are we hiding in Him?

SHADOW OF A GREAT ROCK
IN A WEARY LAND

"And a man shall be as. . .
the shadow of a great rock in a weary land."
Isaiah 32:2

Journeying one night in the wilderness of central Africa in a section plagued by many ravenous beasts, we found no place of safety till we came to the shadow of a great rock, where we sat down with our backs to the rock and, building at our feet a great fire, found rest and refreshing for the next day's still weary journey. O weary child, when thy strength fails and thou canst go no further, sit down and lean back in the shadow of thy Lord, upon Him. Build there in prayer the fire of faith and find rest and refreshment for thine onward march.

AS RIVERS OF WATER
IN A DRY PLACE

"And a man shall be as. . .
rivers of water in a dry place."
Isaiah 32:2

To know the blessing of water in abundance we need to have felt a very keen thirst. Wandering one time in part of Africa's desert, two missionaries traveled without water until thirst became first a pain, then an agony, then almost insanity. After long marching over dry, burning sands they came to the waters of a wide, deep river and quenched their thirst. "If any man thirst let him come unto me," and He is near. No matter how deep our thirst, how great our longing or our need, He who is as "RIVERS OF WATER IN A DRY PLACE" has said, "Lo, I am with you. Drink, and be satisfied."

THE KING IN HIS BEAUTY

"Thine eyes shall see the king in his beauty;
they shall behold the land that is very far off."
Isaiah 33:17

Blessed are the pure in heart, for they shall see God." Do our lives see the King in His beauty? Do we grip the fact that as we gaze upon Him it is His will that we should be changed unto the same likeness, "from glory unto glory"? "A little while and the world seeth me no more, but *ye see me.*" No more wonderful promise is ours for present experiences than this. O Lord, let every mist and veil that hide Thy glory be removed, and every sin be put away, that we may behold Thee in the beauty of holiness. Then "the beauty of the Lord thy God shall be upon thee."

OUR LAWGIVER

"For the LORD is our judge,
the LORD is our lawgiver,
the LORD is our king; he will save us."
Isaiah 33:22

Every nation, every act, every life, needs a law to direct it in its relation to its own expression, and to others. That law must be made by one who knows and understands the nation, act, or life. Jesus is our "LAWGIVER." He who gave us life, He who has lived the life we need to live—He knows. He made the law for us in infinite tenderness and love. "He that hath my commandments and keepeth them, he it is that loveth me."

JEHOVAH

"The voice of one that crieth, Prepare ye
in the wilderness the way of Jehovah;
make level in the desert a highway for our God."
Isaiah 40:3 RV

JEHOVAH—"The Self-existent One who reveals Himself." Into the wilderness of my lost way He comes to find me and lead me out. Into the desert of my barren life enters JEHOVAH and makes all the desert a garden. Into my death He brings His life and to my dead senses reveals Himself The One Eternal God. Shall we pray for greater grace to receive all the revelation of Himself which He would give?

THE LORD JEHOVAH

"Behold, the Lord Jehovah will come as a mighty one,
and His arm will rule for Him; Behold, His reward is
with Him, and His recompense before Him."
Isaiah 40:10 RV

Not every soul that worships Jehovah has learned that the secret of all power and of fullness of blessing is in making Him the Master of our lives. Adonai Jehovah is the Lord, the Ruler, the Master, who in eternal grace reveals Himself. Shall we not humbly bow at His feet and crown Him Lord, Master, of all that we have and are?

THE EVERLASTING GOD

"Hast thou not known? hast thou not heard,
that the everlasting God, the LORD,
the Creator of the ends of the earth,
fainteth not, neither is weary?
There is no searching of his understanding."
Isaiah 40:28

Everlasting, never-ending,
Age-abiding is my Lord.
Never shadow caused by turning,
Changeless, perfect, is His Word.

EVERLASTING GOD, I pray Thee
Steady, strengthen, stablish me.
Safe from grief and pain and failure,
Hide me, Everlasting God, in Thee.

A LIGHT OF THE GENTILES

"I the LORD have called thee in righteousness,
and will. . .give thee. . .for a light of the Gentiles."
Isaiah 42:6

In him was life, and the life was the light of men." But how shall that Light lighten the Gentiles unless we who are the light of the world shall go forth among the Gentiles and let the light shine? Someone brought that

Light to us. Shall we not bear it on a little farther into the darkness of some other life? He *is* the Light. He *gave* the Light. We are the *Light-bearers*.

MINE ELECT

"Behold my servant, whom I uphold,
mine elect, in whom my soul delighteth;
I have put my spirit upon him;
he shall bring forth judgment to the Gentiles."
Isaiah 42:1

Infinite God, who knows and understands, the God of wisdom and of knowledge, called in review all angels and all men of all the ages and of all time and chose our Lord and called Him "MINE ELECT," to be the world's Redeemer, Savior, Friend and the believer's All in All. Does thy choice fall on Him, each day, each hour, in each experience? May He be all in all to thee today.

THE POLISHED SHAFT

"And he hath made my mouth like a sharp sword;
in the shadow of his hand hath he hid me,
and made me a polished shaft."
Isaiah 49:2

In every part of the Word of God our Lord is pictured as the "Word of God" having a "voice as the sound of many waters," and speaking to His people words of peace and comfort and of power. But no name of Christ is more true of Him than that He is a "POLISHED SHAFT," and when He speaks and His word cuts through our

selfish lives like a sword of radiant light, let us rejoice.
The Adversary of our souls would make us proud of
self. Few human friends are faithful, but He who is "A
POLISHED SHAFT" speaks not only with eternal love but
with unchanging faithfulness. *"Speak Lord, for thy servant heareth thee."* Amen.

THE HOLY ONE OF ISRAEL

"Thus saith the Lord, the Redeemer of Israel,
and his Holy One, to him whom man despiseth,
to him whom the nation abhorreth,
to a servant of rulers, Kings shall see and arise,
princes also shall worship,
because of the LORD that is faithful,
and the Holy One of Israel,
and he shall choose thee."
Isaiah 49:7

All Israel walked in sin. All Israel was defiled. And
yet in cloud by day, in fire by night, within the
Holy tabernacle there stood a Presence, Holy, Infinite
in love and grace and power. "THE HOLY ONE OF ISRAEL"
could not forget His chosen people nor resist their
faintest cry. So Israel stood and lived, and lives today
because "THE HOLY ONE OF ISRAEL" stood beside them.
And beside thy soul He stands today to be thy righteousness and lead thee to Himself. Behold Him, and
adore!

A Root Out of a Dry Ground

"For he shall grow up before him as a tender plant,
and as a root out of a dry ground."
Isaiah 53:2

D ear discouraged soul, does it seem sometimes to
thee that thy lot is a hard one? That thou hast been
asked to stand in difficult places and where surrounding
conditions have been most unfavorable? He who
redeemed thee knows every difficulty, every sorrow,
which thou canst feel. Dishonored by ignorant
doubters, He must needs turn even to the wondrous
mother who had received both natural and supernatural
knowledge of His Divine character and mission and
ask, "How is it that ye sought Me? Wist ye not. . . ?" He
hath suffered "in all points like as we" and is, therefore,
"able to succor" us. Then "consider Him who grew up
A Root Out of a Dry Ground" lest ye grow weary and
faint in your minds.

A Man of Sorrows

"He is despised and rejected of men;
a man of sorrows, and acquainted with grief;
and we hid as it were our faces from him;
he was despised and we esteemed him not."
Isaiah 53:3

H e who was the source of all joy, the giver of all
peace, He before whom angels and archangels bow
in adoration, is also called a "Man of Sorrows." Grief
broke His heart, crushed out His life. Shall we through

disobedience, rebellion, or lack of love or service or worship, add to the sorrows which He bore, or shall we murmur if we too shall be permitted to partake of His sorrows, or to share His grief? He sorrowed all alone, save perhaps as angels ministered to Him in Gethsemane's deep shadow. But He shares thy grief, He carries all thy sorrow and comforts those who trust in Him. Shall we not worship and adore the MAN OF SORROWS?

MY MAKER

"For thy Maker is thine husband."
Isaiah 54:5

We hear of "self-made men," of men who are made by their surroundings, or by devoted friends and fellows. How rarely do we hear today the humble, joyful boast, "By the grace of God I am what I am." And yet "He is thy MAKER"! All thou art that is lasting, all thou art that is good, all thou art that is helpful, God has made. Bow then before thy MAKER. Worship and petition Him to finish that which He began.

MY RIGHTEOUS SERVANT

"He shall see of the travail of his soul,
and shall be satisfied; by his knowledge
shall my righteous servant justify many;
for he shall bear their iniquities."
Isaiah 53:11

There are many servants, only *One* is righteous. Paul was able to say, "I have declared unto you the whole counsel of God, I have fought a good fight, I have kept the faith," but still must call himself an unprofitable servant, and less than the least of all saints. Shall we therefore become discouraged and conclude that it is not worthwhile to try? Nay, "your labor is not in vain in the Lord," for He who was "MY RIGHTEOUS SERVANT shall justify many." For He is still "Jehovah Tsidkenu," (our Righteousness), and we may bring the dropped stitches of our best weaving, and the broken efforts of our best service, and laying all at His feet rejoice that we are justified by Him who is "God's Righteous Servant."

THE GOD OF
THE WHOLE EARTH

"The Lord of Hosts is his name;
and thy Redeemer the Holy One of Israel;
the God of the whole earth shall he be called."
Isaiah 54:5

Is there any part of the earth that is mine? Not till I am truly a child of "THE GOD OF THE WHOLE EARTH." May I not receive Him and possess all things in Christ and proceed to enjoy them, untroubled by the world's woe? Not till the whole earth has heard that He is "The God," not of a few, but "of the whole earth."

A Witness to the People

"Behold, I have given him for a witness to the people,
a leader and commander to the people."
Isaiah 55:4

A witness of the love of God, the grace, the power, the holiness of Deity. No flaw in all that matchless testimony, no doubtful, double-meaning speech, and He could say, "He that hath seen me hath seen the Father." We too are *witnesses,* but oh, how full of flaws is all our testimony! The Father dwelt with Him and He sought the Father's guidance at every step and every word. We too may see and hear and walk with God, and so alone shall our witness win the wanderers home.

A Commander

"Behold, I have given him for a. . .
commander to the people."
Isaiah 55:4

In a day when nearly every man desires to do that which is right in his own eyes, it becomes difficult for all God's children to recognize His right to command. Yet He who redeemed us, who bought us so that we are not our own, proclaimed His right to the title of "Commander." Failure to obey will account for most of the loss of communion and joy in prayer and in the study of God's Word. If there be any commandment which He has brought home to our hearts which we have not obeyed, shall we not today grant Him instant, cheerful, loving obedience, and make Him in every detail of life our Commander?

THE REDEEMER

*"And the Redeemer shall come to Zion, and unto them
that turn from transgression in Jacob, saith the Lord."*
Isaiah 59:20

When failure comes and disappointment, when thy
soul has been defeated and the race seems hopeless, stop and think "thy Lord redeemed thee and at
countless cost." If He saw in thee that for which to pay
His life, Himself, His all, is it not worth while to rise and
try again, walking with Him and worshiping Him who
redeemed thee?

A LEADER

*"Behold, I have given him for. . .
a leader and commander to the people."*
Isaiah 55:4

From the beginning of our Christian lives the fact that
"He leadeth me" is one of the most blessed thoughts
that comes to a child of God. But we think most often of
His leading to battle, leading out of the mazes of confusion and ignorance, leading through the darkness of our
night. Do we realize that infinite tenderness that makes
Him gently lead those who are doing the finest and the
most difficult and unknown service of the world? The
sorrow, the loneliness, the pain, which no friend on earth
can know, He understands, He feels with us, and gently
leads us through the shadows to His own great glory.
Shall we not follow where He leads, and keep so close
to Him that we shall never miss the way?

THINE EVERLASTING LIGHT

"Thy sun shall no more go down;
neither shall thy moon withdraw itself:
for the LORD shall be thine everlasting light,
and the days of thy mourning shall be ended."
Isaiah 60:20

No picture is more difficult for us to spiritually apprehend than a time when the sun shall no more go down. When Christ shall be to us "EVERLASTING LIGHT." Our lives are so filled with ups and downs, with lights and shadows, that stability seems almost inconceivable, and everlasting darkness easier to understand than everlasting light. Yet such is Christ to thee. Then enter in with holy boldness and walk in EVERLASTING LIGHT.

THE ANGEL OF
HIS PRESENCE

"In all their affliction he was afflicted,
and the angel of his presence saved them;
in his love and in his pity he redeemed them;
and he bare them and carried them
all the days of old."
Isaiah 63:9

A nervous, restless boy, in his early childhood, called out again and again in the night, "Daddy, are you there?" The father answered, "Yes, I am here. Do you want anything?" "No, I only wanted to be sure you were there." And the frightened boy, still in the dark, went directly to sleep. Oh, child of God, beset by fears and troubled so that thou hast found no rest, let "THE ANGEL OF HIS PRESENCE" comfort thee. Unstop thy ears. Speak to Him, and thou shalt hear the voice of Him who spake as never man spake, saying "Lo, I am with thee."

OUR POTTER

"But now, O LORD,
thou art our father;
we are the clay, and thou our potter;
and we all are the work of thy hand."
Isaiah 64:8

Have you understood the meaning of the force that presses in upon your life today? Has it seemed only pain, only wrong and deep injustice? Back of all that seems to be, the POTTER *stands,* with an ideal so lofty that our highest imagination has not fully grasped it. A beauteous, transformed life, fit to sit with Him upon His throne, is in the POTTER'S mind, and He is shaping thee through that which seemed a rude experience. Shall we not learn to say today, *"I am the clay, and Thou* THE POTTER. *Shape me as Thou wilt, dear Lord."* Amen.

BALM OF GILEAD

"Is there no balm in Gilead?"
Jeremiah 8:22

There are experiences of suffering through which the Master wills that we should pass. There are burdens which He does not lift, though He takes us, burden and all, into His everlasting arms. But in every suffering which He permits, He is our "BALM." He eases every pain. He comforts every sorrow. He strengthens us in every weakness. There is a "Balm" in our Gilead. Shall we take from Him the comfort which He offers us today?

MY PORTION

"The portion of Jacob is not like them; for he is the former of all things and Israel is the rod of his inheritance; The LORD of hosts is his name."
Jeremiah 10:16

When we are able to lay hold of the fact that Jesus is "OUR PORTION," then do we truly possess all things, for "how shall he not with him freely give us all things?" Nay, more, "For all things are yours. Whether Paul, or Apollos, or Cephas, or the world, or life, or death, or things present, or things to come, all are yours. And ye are Christ's and Christ is God's." Shall we seek to appropriate all of His matchless love and grace and hope and courage and joy and fruit and power? What more can we ask, or have?

THE HOPE OF ISRAEL

"O, the hope of Israel,
the saviour thereof in time of trouble,
why shouldest thou be as a stranger in the land,
and as a wayfaring man that turneth
aside to tarry for a night?"
Jeremiah 14:8

THE HOPE OF HIS PEOPLE," Israel, is also the Hope of His Bride, the church. Israel shall be regathered and become, though now despised of man and all nations, the chiefest kingdom in all the earth. And when He shall come He shall be both "HOPE" and full fruition to every believing soul. *"Even so come, Lord Jesus, come quickly."* Amen.

MY PHYSICIAN

"Is there no balm in Gilead;
is there no physician there?
Why then is not the health of the daughter
of my people recovered?"
Jeremiah 8:22

Dr. Arthur T. Pierson once said in a sermon preached in London, England, that one of the marked proofs of our failure to live up to the light we have, is found in our failure to obey the commandment in James' epistle, "Is any among you sick? Let him call for the elders of the church and pray over him." We rush at once to secure human aid, forgetting even to pray as we go, or that He who formed us and through whose blessing alone the human means can be effective, is "OUR PHYSICIAN."

A Righteous Branch

"Behold, the days come, saith the Lord,
that I will raise unto David a righteous Branch,
and a King shall reign and prosper,
and shall execute judgment and justice in the earth."
Jeremiah 23:5

A "righteous servant" is one who serves righteously, satisfying every command of his master. A "righteous branch" is one which rightly respects, honors, and bears fruit to the tree from which it grows. "Ye are branches," our Savior said of us, but He also said, "My Father pruneth." He who is the RIGHTEOUS BRANCH heard the Father say, "This is my beloved Son in whom I am well pleased." Shall we not seek with all our hearts to so abide in Him that we shall glorify the Father by bearing much fruit?

David, Their King

"But they shall serve the LORD their God,
and David their king,
whom I will raise up unto them."
Jeremiah 30:9

What doubt, what incredulity of men has blinded human eyes lest they should see that David, Israel's King, shall truly be raised up unto them! How much we lose of deep reality, of wondrous truth and vivid picture in the Word of God because our eyes are holden through our unbelief. How beautiful, how wonderful, that Christ our coming Lord should call Himself

"DAVID, THEIR KING." What are our thoughts and prayers concerning Israel? Are we seeking, hoping for their King and telling them that He is our King too? And praying that their eyes may be anointed to behold in Christ, "DAVID, THEIR KING"!

RESTING PLACE

"My people hath been lost sheep;
their shepherds have caused them to go astray,
they have turned them away on the mountains:
they have gone from mountain to hill,
they have forgotten their resting place."
Jeremiah 50:6

Truly there is rest for the weary, for Jesus is "OUR RESTING PLACE." Therefore, in the midst of the toil and the weariness, in the midst of the struggle and strife, let us ask that our ears may be opened to hear Him who said, "Come unto me, all ye who labor and are heavy laden, and I will give you rest." To abide in Him in continuous love and obedient faith is to find Him "OUR RESTING PLACE."

THE SHEPHERD OF ISRAEL

"And I will set up one shepherd over them. . .
and he shall be their shepherd."
Ezekiel 34:23

Is any name more comforting to weary, needy children of our God than Jesus' name of Shepherd? Feeding, leading beside still water, watching over all our wanderings, bringing us as the SHEPHERD OF ISRAEL brought His flock out of the wilderness over the Jordan into the land of peace and plenty. *Teach us to trust in Thee, O* SHEPHERD OF ISRAEL. *Amen.*

FEEDER

"And I will set up one shepherd over them,
and he shall feed them, even my servant David:
he shall feed them, and he shall be their shepherd."
Ezekiel 34:23

The lie of the Adversary to God's children is always that they are "lost." Or that "difficulty is a sign that God has ceased to know or care." When we have wandered from Him, from right, from rest, from peace, "He restoreth my soul." It is His self-appointed task—the work which love makes a necessity for Him, as well as for His wandering sheep.

"How gentle God's commands,
How kind His precepts are."

What He feeds is as important for us to learn as *when* and *where.* So let us cultivate our appetite, our longing, for His righteousness, and we shall find He is "OUR FEEDER."

A STONE CUT WITHOUT HANDS

"Thou sawest till that a stone was cut out without hands, which smote the image upon his feet that were of iron and clay, and brake them to pieces. . . and the stone that smote the image became a great mountain, and filled the whole earth."
Daniel 2:34, 35

Men plan for peace in human governments, build courts of arbitration, leagues of nations, pacts and pledges, only to find them crumbling in utter failure before the human work is half complete. The Eternal God is planning a kingdom and government that cannot fail, and He the King, whose shape and form and size and power are ordered by the Most High God, will smite in His coming every man-made plan. Are we looking for that "STONE" to come and smite? Shall we be "ready in the day of His power"?

A PLANT OF RENOWN

"And I will raise up for them a plant of renown, and they shall be no more consumed with hunger in the land neither bear the shame of the heathen any more."
Ezekiel 34:29

Although our Lord came as a tender plant, and with no form nor comeliness, yet has He become a PLANT OF RENOWN, for already no other name is so widely known, no other name carries such wondrous power, no other name shows such boundless grace, and sometime, perhaps soon, "every knee shall bow and every tongue proclaim" that "the tender plant" is a "PLANT OF RENOWN," that "Jesus Christ is Lord to the glory of God the Father."

THE HOPE OF HIS PEOPLE

"The LORD also shall roar out of Zion,
and utter his voice from Jerusalem;
and the heavens and the earth shall shake;
but the LORD will be the hope of his people,
and the strength of the children of Israel."
Joel 3:16

There is no hope apart from Him; no hope in self to win against the world, the flesh and the Devil! No hope in self to either be or do that which shall bless the world; but there is glorious hope for those who trust in Him. Jesus who is our Savior, King and Bridegroom, the Living Head of the Body of which we are but humble members, "He is THE HOPE OF HIS PEOPLE." He it is that "worketh in me both to will and to do."

WALL OF FIRE

"For I, saith the Lord,
will be unto her a wall of fire round about,
and will be the glory in the midst of her."
Zechariah 2:5

All the defense that we need is God to those who trust in Him. A WALL OF FIRE through which the fiercest foe can never come. The foe of evil thoughts will be burned. The hasty tongue will be consumed. The selfish desire that creeps so insidiously through every other barricade will be consumed by Him who is a "WALL OF FIRE" when we shall hide in Him.

THE ANCIENT OF DAYS

*"I saw in the night visions, and, behold, one like the
Son of man came with the clouds of heaven,
and came to the Ancient of days, and they brought
him near before him. . . . his dominion is an
everlasting dominion, which shall not pass away,
and his kingdom that which shall not be destroyed."*
Daniel 7:13,14

In the beginning was the Word," and He who redeemed us is "THE ANCIENT OF DAYS," "whose head is white as snow" (Revelation 1:14). He was from everlasting and will be unto the ages of ages our Eternal God. Shall not we, whose life upon the earth is but a hand-breadth, bow in worship and adoration at the feet of "THE ANCIENT OF DAYS"?

THE PRINCE OF PRINCES

*"He shall also stand up against the Prince of princes;
but he shall be broken without hand."*
Daniel 8:25

By every word which men could understand Almighty God has sought to exalt His Son, so that in all things He might have the preeminence in our lives, as King of kings, as Lord of lords, and as in this text, "THE PRINCE OF PRINCES." In earthly kingdoms it is very often true that upon the prince who is heir apparent to the throne is lavished more affection than upon the King himself. What about our love and affection to "THE PRINCE OF PRINCES"? Although sitting now at the right hand of the Father and one with Him, He is waiting to be crowned on earth. Do we pay Him more devotion and deeper love than we do to these erring mortals who reign over us? Let us, in the real things of daily life, exalt Him to His rightful place and pour out our devotion to Him.

RULER

"But thou, Bethlehem Ephratah,
though thou be little among the thousands of Judah,
yet out of thee shall he come forth unto me
that is to be ruler in Israel;
whose goings forth have been from of old,
from everlasting."
Micah 5:2

Never in the history of the world has there been such hopeless failure of human governments as now. Never such high ideals, and never have high ideals fallen so flat. Great plans are made and conferences held to promote peace and good government, and like flimsy houses of cards the highest hopes are shattered in ruthless, heartless, brutal war. So must it be until He who has the right to reign shall come and be "RULER," not alone in Israel, but in all the world. More than thirty years ago one who was a chosen spokesman of the Lord said, "Perhaps He would have come sooner if we had, from our hearts, prayed more earnestly, 'Thy Kingdom come.'" Do we ask it and sincerely desire it?

STRONG HOLD

"The LORD is good,
a strong hold in the day of trouble;
and he knoweth them that trust in him."
Nahum 1:7

During the late terrible war when the huge flying craft sailed over London, multitudes of people hid in the subways of London. In the Highlands of Central Africa there is a section know as "The Iron Stone Plateau," where the amount of ore appears to attract the lightning, and many adventurers in that section stopping long at a place, dig cellars into which they go when thunderstorms arise. There are dangerous storms which beset our spiritual life from which there is no safe retreat but Christ. Is He your "STRONG HOLD"? Have you learned to hide in Him?

MY SERVANT, THE BRANCH

"Hear now, O Joshua the high priest,
thou, and thy fellows that sit before thee;
for they are men wondered at; for, behold,
I will bring forth my servant the BRANCH."
Zechariah 3:8

No lesson, not even that of courage, is more often repeated, and perhaps none is more often needed, than the lesson given us in our Lord's humility. He upon whose shoulders the Father lay all government; He who is the Mighty God; He who, "even when He subsisted in the form of God," "made Himself of no reputation" and became not only the Branch, but "My Servant," and in doing this has marked the pathway for every child of God. Are you God's servant, serving Him as your only Master, doing joyfully and eagerly His will? If in aught you have sought to follow any other master, will you submit your life, your *all* to Him, and be His Servant now?

King Over All the Earth

"And His feet shall stand in that day
upon the mount of Olives, . . .
And the Lord my God shall come,
and all the saints with thee. . .
And the Lord shall be king over all the earth;
in that day shall there be one Lord,
and his name one."
Zechariah 14:4, 5, 9

Some day, God grant it may be soon, "His feet shall stand upon the Mount of Olives" and all the Earth shall know that He is King. Can any flight of swift imagination exceed that picture? Through all the strife of nations, all the pride and rivalry of kings, what peace, what glory, what undreamed of wonders shall be seen when He, "The King of kings," shall reign "over all the Earth." Does that day not allure you? Does not the Spirit-given cry fill at your soul—"Even so, come, Lord Jesus!"

THE BRANCH

*"And speak unto him saying, Thus speaketh the
LORD of hosts, saying, Behold the man whose name is
The BRANCH; and he shall grow up out of his place,
and he shall build the temple of the Lord."*
Zechariah 6:12

While He was here on earth THE BRANCH said, "The
Son can do nothing of himself, but what he seeth
the Father do," taking the place of humility in His utter
dependence upon God the Father. Are we tempted to exalt
ourselves, to work in some strength which He has given
in the past? Let us bow at His feet and remember that
except "ye abide in me ye can do nothing." Let us consider Him who, although He was the Mighty God, yet
called Himself in His earthly relationship "THE BRANCH."

JEHOVAH MY GOD

*"And ye shall flee by the valley of my mountains. . .
and Jehovah my God shall come,
and all the holy ones with thee."*
Zechariah 14:5 RV

The Self-Existing One, seeking ever to reveal Himself to His children and to the world that knows
Him not, is pleased and glorified when that revelation
leads our souls to cry, "JEHOVAH, MY GOD." If "that
thing or person who most absorbs our thought is our
God," then who is my God today? The matchless
Jehovah? Or some other being or created thing, unwor-
thy of my trust and worship? Let us not rest until from
our inmost soul we cry, "JEHOVAH, MY GOD."

The King

"And it shall come to pass that every one that is left of all the nations which came against Jerusalem, shall even go up from year to year to worship the King, the LORD of hosts, and to keep the feast of tabernacles."
Zechariah 14:16

He is King, it matters not that earth refused to crown Him and to acknowledge His right to reign. He only waits the Father's day and hour to receive the kingdom which is His. The world waits and weeps, the whole creation groans in pain for lack of the conditions that shall be when men have crowned Him KING. We join that grief, but have we truly crowned Him in our lives? Does He reign supremely every day, in every act, and rule our words and thoughts? There will be joy in His heart, joy in Heaven, and joy in your heart, when you shall fully and with no reserve crown Jesus King and Lord of All.

The Messenger of the Covenant

"Behold, I will send my Messenger. . . even the messenger of the covenant, whom ye delight in; behold he shall come, saith the LORD of hosts."
Malachi 3:1

He who is our example that we should walk in His steps has called Himself "THE MESSENGER OF THE COVENANT." The Father gave a promise to those who should believe in His Son. The Son came bringing that promise, that covenant—a Messenger sent from Heaven. To the true believer that most precious covenant is, "I will write my laws upon their hearts, and upon their minds will I engrave them." Will you accept it now? "Open thy mouth wide and I will fill it."

PURIFIER

"And He shall sit as a. . .purifier of silver."
Malachi 3:3

No work of God shows more plainly His boundless love than His desire to purify our lives. So much of dross is found in us that we have need to be tried in the furnace of affliction and to be purged as gold and silver. The difficult experiences through which we pass may often be understood as the infinite love of the Father, seeking to separate the dross from our lives, to bring us to a point of purity where we may see and reflect His image.

JESUS CHRIST

"The book of the generation of Jesus Christ."
Matthew 1:1

Here is the first title given to our Lord in the New Testament—Jesus Christ. This chapter contains a host of names, covering three periods of fourteen generations each, but *one Name* stands out like a radiant star to lighten all the others; *one Person* to whom all must render allegiance,—Jesus (Savior) Christ (the Anointed

One). At His feet every knee shall bow in heaven and on earth. *Let us pour out our hearts to Him in praise and in prayer this day, and every day. Amen.*

SON OF ABRAHAM

*"The book of the generation of Jesus Christ. . .
the Son of Abraham."*
Matthew 1:1

Three titles in one verse, "Jesus Christ—Son of David —Son of Abraham." Abraham was the head of the covenant nation. God had given to him the promise that in his seed should all the nations of the earth be blessed. Jesus submitted to the Jewish law in righteousness. He lived as a Jew, He preached to the Jews. He died for the Jews as well as for all people. "So then, they which be of faith are blessed with faithful Abraham" (Galatians 3:9). How wonderful God manifested in the flesh as Abraham's seed and yet the One who made the promise to Abraham! *Oh, Thou promised* SON OF ABRAHAM *and Son of God, our Savior, hold us fast in faith in Thy Word. Amen.*

REFINER

*"And he shall sit as a refiner and purifier of silver:
and he shall purify the sons of Levi, and purge them
as gold and silver, that they may offer unto the LORD
an offering in righteousness."*
Malachi 3:3

When grosser things which men can see are re-moved from our lives, there is grave danger that we shall be satisfied and forget that still as the Heaven is high above the earth, so high are His ways above our ways, and His thoughts above our thoughts. That there is a finer life, a deeper, holier peace, a clearer, surer likeness of the Lord possible for His children, needs to be apprehended. And though through all of life we may seem to have been in the melting pot, shall we not say to Him again at any cost, "Dear REFINER, make me what Thou wilt. Refine me by any process that seemeth good unto Thee."

JESUS

"Thou shalt call his name JESUS;
for he shall save his people from their sins."
Matthew 1:21

Over seven hundred times in the New Testament is this name used—"JESUS" (Joshua). How familiar we are with that name! Joshua of the Old Testament, who saved Israel by leading them through the River Jordan, fought their battles, and was steadfast in his allegiance to God and His people. He was a type of our Lord who is our Joshua; who fights our battles for us; who is our Leader, our Protector, our Savior! Who will never cease His lordship until He has us safely in the sheepfold on the other side. Hallelujah, what a Savior! *This day, Thou Savior of our souls, in whom we are separated for eternity, guide us by Thy Holy Spirit to the praise of Thy grace. Amen.*

THE SON OF DAVID

"The book of the generation of Jesus Christ,
the Son of David."
Matthew 1:1

Our Lord was a lineal descendant of David, the king. This entitled Him to the right of sovereignty over David's land, and when He was here among men, we are told, there was no other claimant to the throne of David. Herod sought to destroy the Child-King, Jesus, but Egypt was chosen as a refuge place for Him. The heart of Herod was like the hearts of all the children of men who will not have Him to rule over them. He was bearing us upon His heart, as a Child, for He is the same "yesterday, today and forever," and He is our refuge now. *Jesus Christ,* SON OF DAVID, *may our hearts be linked up with Thy great heart always. Amen.*

EMMANUEL

"Behold, a virgin. . .shall bring forth a son,
and they shall call his name Emmanuel."
Matthew 1:23

This was the prophecy of Isaiah 7:14: "Therefore, the Lord himself shall give you a sign; Behold a virgin shall conceive, and bear a son, and shall call his name Immanuel." "EMMANUEL" (God with us)! What a wonderful God and Savior He is and He is with us as He promised in Matthew 28:19, 20: "Go ye, therefore, and teach all nations, baptizing them in the name of the Father, and of the Son, and of the Holy Ghost. Teaching them to observe all things whatsoever I have commanded you; and, lo, I am with you alway, even unto the end of the age." Let us sense His presence and make Him real. Walk, talk, live with, and love Him more and more as the days go by. *Lord Jesus, we know that Thou dwellest in us. May we enjoy Thy fellowship today. Amen.*

THE YOUNG CHILD

"When they had heard the king, they departed; and, lo, the star, which they saw in the east, went before them, till it came and stood over where the young child was."
Matthew 2:9

A star in the East led the Wise Men to a Star that shall outshine all the stars of Heaven. Look at this YOUNG CHILD! Hold fast your attention as you gaze upon His face, lying there, His eyes looking into your own inquiring eyes. Visualize, if you can, God manifested in the flesh for you. God—the YOUNG CHILD! The Creator of all things! Before whom are thirty years of human life in which He will toil with His fellow men. Mystery of mysteries! *Oh, Thou wonderful One, as we bow before Thee today, help us to discern something of Thy devotion for the sons of men. Amen.*

A GOVERNOR

"And thou Bethlehem. . .out of thee shall come a Governor, that shall rule my people, Israel."
Matthew 2:6

B ethlehem of Judah! A little village, twice highly honored! The birthplace of David, king of Israel, and the birthplace of Jesus the Christ, King of kings and Lord of lords! Who could visit this Land of Promise and not desire to see this city of cities, the place where Jehovah enthroned in human form and lying in a manger gazed into the face of the virgin Mary, His mother. The government shall be upon His shoulders and He will reign in righteousness. Blessed day! *We pray for its soon coming, and ask for grace that we may hasten it. Amen.*

FRIEND OF SINNERS

"Behold. . .a friend of publicans and sinners."
Matthew 11:19

These are the words of Jesus Himself. He quotes their own phrases as applied to Himself. What a title! How wonderfully true it is—"A FRIEND OF SINNERS!" So He was and so He is—a Friend that sticketh closer than a brother. Laying aside the royal robes of Heaven, he came here to befriend sinful men. It was a life-work that cost Him His life. Hallelujah! What a Friend! How gladly He paid the price of friendship. As we take up the work of the day, let us ask ourselves the question, "Am I a friend of sinners?" If not, then I am not like my Lord, for He was and He joyed in it. *Lord Jesus, the world is full of friendless sinners. May we make them acquainted with Thee who art their Friend. Amen.*

A Nazarene

*"And he came and dwelt in a city called Nazareth;
that it might be fulfilled which was spoken by the
prophets, He shall be called a Nazarene."*
Matthew 2:23

Nazareth was a town in the northern border of the
plain of Esdraelon. Here came the angel Gabriel
and announced to Mary the coming birth of Christ:
"And the angel came in unto her, and said, Hail, thou
that art highly favoured, the Lord is with thee; blessed
art thou among women" (Luke 1:26-28). On the night
of His betrayal our Lord asked the question, "Whom
seek ye?" They replied, "Jesus of Nazareth" and He
said, "I am He." *Jesus of Nazareth, may we never be
ashamed to be called the followers of the lowly
Nazarene.*

The Servant of Jehovah

"Behold my servant, whom I have chosen."
Matthew 12:18

Jesus, the prophesied Servant! Isaiah had portrayed
Him. Jehovah had chosen Him. All of God's ways
were known unto Him from the beginning. You hear the
echo of His voice, "I delight to do thy will, O my God!"
Nothing was too great for Him to do, for He was the
Creator, and nothing was too hard for Him, for He had
all power. Nothing was too small for Him to do, for He
stooped to notice a widow's mite and give a mighty lesson from it. What a gracious privilege to be yoked with
Him in service. *Dear Lord, let us labor with Thee, the*

"Servant of Jehovah," *today and thus make it a good day for Thee. Amen.*

My Beloved

"Behold. . .my beloved,
in whom my soul is well pleased."
Matthew 12:18

Twenty-seven times in the Song of Solomon is this title used of our Lord. God's Son was a beloved Servant. How dear He was to the Father—dear as the apple of His eye. Yet His love for us was manifest in the surrender of His Son to pay the penalty of our sin. "Greater love hath no man than this." "While we were yet sinners, Christ died for us." In the hour of darkness He cried, "My God, my God, why hast thou forsaken me?" The agony, the grief, the pain He suffered, all had a voice which rings out the message, "God so loved." *Our Father, Thy love for us has broken all the barriers down; and we pray that Thy Spirit may rest upon us this day as we meditate upon the greatness of Thy love. Amen.*

A Sower

"He that soweth the good seed is the Son of man."
Matthew 13:37

The seed is the Word of God. God's Son sowed the good seed. He soweth the Word of Truth in the hearts of men. When we sow the Gospel we sow good seed. When we give out the Word of God we are sowing good seed. Nothing is comparable to the *Word* itself. It has potential power. It is a *living* seed and never fails. We are to imitate our Lord, the SOWER, and see that the pure seed of the Word is scattered wherever we go. "Sow beside all waters." *Lord, make me a seed-sower this day, and hear my prayer for all the sowers in all the world. Amen!*

THE CHRIST

"Thou art the Christ, the Son of the living God."
Matthew 16:16

This is the title of the long-looked-for Savior—the Anointed One. Prophets had foretold His coming and now His kingly authority is recorded. Over three hundred times is this title used in the New Testament. From "CHRIST" comes the word, "Christian," and from "Christian" comes the word, "Christianity." Today this land of ours is the foremost Christian nation of the world. Our Gospel is the Gospel of Christ of which we are not ashamed, for it is the power of God unto salvation to everyone that believeth. *Lord, as "Christ-ones" let us honor Thee by having the same anointing power resting upon us as we enter the service of the day. Amen.*

THE PROPHET OF NAZARETH

"This is Jesus the prophet of Nazareth of Galilee."
Matthew 21:11

This great demonstration had been planned by God and foretold by Him (Zechariah 9:9). Our Lord comes into Jerusalem riding upon the foal of an ass. The crowd is vast; the enthusiasm is great. "Who is this?" is the cry; and the answer is, "This is Jesus, THE PROPHET OF NAZARETH." A despised Nazarene! A prophet from an obscure village! We are all proud if, perchance, we were born in some noted place; but God, when He took the form of a man, was born in a manger and made His home in Nazareth. For our sakes He became poor, that we through His poverty, might be made rich. *Let us meditate upon the riches of His grace, bow at His feet and kiss them as we adore Him; and may we walk humbly this day with the despised Nazarene. Amen.*

JESUS THE CHRIST

"Then charged he his disciples that they should tell no man that he was Jesus the Christ."
Matthew 16:20

This title, "Jesus the Christ," is used a hundred times in the New Testament. "The Savior—the Anointed One"—a combination that magnifies the office of the One whom we long to worship. The time had not yet come for them to preach the story of redemption. They were to hold their peace for a season, but He tells us to go into all the world and tell to all people the wonderful message of Jesus Christ and His finished work. Are we obeying the command? *Dear Father, as we go forth today with this precious Name in our hearts and on our lips, help us to tell someone of the wonders of the Man, Thy Son, JESUS THE CHRIST! Amen.*

My Beloved Son

"This is my beloved Son, in whom I am
well pleased; hear ye him."
Matthew 17:5

Wonderful manifestation! A cloud of glory over-shadowing that which was too deep for human eyes to penetrate. The voice of Jehovah attesting that Jesus was HIS BELOVED SON and that His words were to be heard. The same voice and the same message were heard in chapter 3, verse 17 when our Lord was baptized, and once again in John 12:28 in the Garden. "His beloved" and our beloved! How marvellous is that testimony to Him whom we have learned to love, and because we love Him, we are beloved of the Father. *Lord, may we breathe it over and over again today, "I am my beloved's and my beloved is mine."* Amen.

Master

"One is your Master, even Christ;
and all ye are brethren."
Matthew 23:8

Master" here means "Teacher," or some say, "Leader." The admonition is to avoid the desire for personal distinction so common among God's leaders. Let our eyes be fixed upon Him and depend upon the Holy Spirit who represents Him, and who guides us into all truth (John 16:13,14). The more we seek to exalt Him, the less will we think of magnifying ourselves. Make Him MASTER of your life today, remembering that

"The disciple is not above his master; but everyone that is perfect shall be as his master" (Luke 6:40). *O, that we may be as our* MASTER, *the meek and lowly One! For this day, our Lord, we need great grace as we seek to follow Thee as* MASTER. *Amen.*

THE BRIDEGROOM

"And while they went to buy, the bridegroom came."
Matthew 25:10

THE BRIDEGROOM must come. The true church is His beloved espoused bride. He has waited a long, long time for her to prepare herself for the glad day and to add the last one which will complete the body. Are you thinking of Him today as the Coming One? And of yourself as one of those who are to be blessed as His beloved throughout eternity? How insignificant are all the little cares and trials! How small they seem when our eyes are turned with expectancy toward Him as He comes in the clouds. "Blessed are they which are called unto the marriage supper of the Lamb" (Revelation 19:9). Hallelujah! *May our prayer always be, "Even so, come, Lord Jesus, come quickly." Amen.*

THE HOLY ONE OF GOD

"I know thee who thou art, the Holy One of God."
Mark 1:24

WHAT a testimony coming from the lips of one possessed of an unclean spirit, Satan's tool, under his power. But the presence of Christ overawed him.

"I know Thee who Thou art, THE HOLY ONE OF GOD."
This was not a willing testimony, but was forced from
him. Many men are devil-possessed, and the devil has
powers accorded him, but Christ can hinder his followers; can cast out his demons and forbid their speaking
(verse 34). How lovingly we should bow at His feet—
the Holy One of God! May we fix our thoughts upon
Him and say many times today as we walk and talk
with Him, *"Oh Thou Holy One of God, glorify Thyself
through us."* Amen.

OUR BROTHER

*"For whosoever shall do the will of God,
the same is my brother."*
Mark 3:35

If this is true, and it is, then the reverse is also true,
and He is our BROTHER. The picture is given in the
thirty-first and thirty-fourth verses: "There came then
his brethren and his mother, and, standing without, sent
unto him, calling him. . . And he looked round about on
them which sat about him, and said, Behold my mother
and my brethren." How wonderful that He should gra-
ciously give this title to those who do the Father's will!
And what is that will? The acceptance of His Son as our
Savior and Lord, and the submission of our will to His
will as revealed in His Word, for His Word is His will.
How near and dear He is to us, our Lord and our
BROTHER! Hold it fast in your meditation—"Ours by
faith; ours forever." *Dear Lord, keep us in loving fellowship with Thyself this day. Amen.*

THOU SON OF THE MOST HIGH GOD

"And cried with a loud voice, and said, What have I do with thee, Jesus, thou Son of the most high God?"
Mark 5:7

Here we are confronted with another testimony from an unclean spirit—"SON OF THE MOST HIGH GOD," he calls Jesus. What unseen powers compelled this significant title? Was it brought about by being face to face with Himself? Judas betrayed Him, but this poor, demon-possessed man worshiped Him. In these strange days many teachers, professors, and preachers refuse to honor Him as the Son, but only as a Son of God. But we lift our hearts to him and say, *"Son of the most high God, be our companion this day and may we withhold naught from Thee."* Amen.

THE CARPENTER

"Is not this the carpenter?"
Mark 6:3

THE CARPENTER! Two things are suggested in this verse. Joseph is not mentioned and is probably not now living. Jesus is working at the carpenter's bench and continued to do so until He assumed His place in His public ministry. We can and should visualize Him in His daily tasks—a man among men. How near He seems to us! What a joy to know that He handled the hammer and sharpened the saw, planed the plank and helped to supply the food for the family. Test this picture of Him with any false system and observe the contrast. No matter what our calling may be, THE CARPENTER will be one with us. We can walk arm in arm with Him to the daily task. *O, Thou Carpenter of Galilee, be Thou our ideal always! Amen.*

SON OF MARY

"Is not this. . .the son of Mary?"
Mark 6:3

The Carpenter, the "SON OF MARY," has come back to His home town from an evangelistic trip in which He had worked many miracles. The people were astonished at His teaching. Prejudice possessed them. "Is not this the SON OF MARY?" We never worship Mary as do our Catholic friends, but we do honor her above all women—God's chosen vessel to bring forth His Son and fulfill His prophecy. How true He was to the last. See Him on the cross and hear His last words to Mary, "Woman, behold thy son" (John, the beloved, to whom He had said, "Behold thy mother"). *Blessed title*—SON OF MARY! *The Babe who is one day to rule the world and at whose feet we shall bow in worshipful adoration! Let us do so now. Amen.*

GOOD MASTER

"Good Master, what shall I do that I may inherit eternal life?"
Mark 10:17

This question was asked of our Lord by a young man with great possessions, as recorded in Matthew 19:17.

This is the concrete question of the soul of man, "What shall I *do* to secure a right to Heaven?" The theme of *religion* is *do;* but the theme of our Lord was just the opposite, "Follow Me." Eternal life is a gift. Those who accept and follow Him find that He *is* the "GOOD MASTER" because He is the "God-Master," for only One is good and He is God, and He has provided for us a salvation—simple to accept but costing Him a price which involved His own life. How gracious is our God and how we should love and adore Him! *Lord, may we walk in the sunshine of Thy love today. Amen.*

SON OF MAN

"The Son of man shall be delivered
unto the chief priests and unto the scribes;
and they shall condemn him to death."
Mark 10:33

In the ninth chapter Jesus had said, "The SON OF MAN is delivered into the hands of men and they shall kill him." How earnestly He sought to stress the fact of His approaching sacrifice upon His disciples and how He longed for their sympathy; but, alas, alas, how hard is the human heart! How difficult it is for Him to win us to Himself! "The SON OF MAN must suffer many things," He had said, but the saddest of all was the failure of His own beloved disciples to enter into the burden He bore as He approached the cross. *Oh, Thou Holy SON OF MAN, give unto us the loving hearts that will enter into fellowship with Thee in all things. Amen.*

A RANSOM

*"The son of man came. . .
to give his life a ransom for many."*
Mark 10:45

A RANSOM for many!" Here Christ is set forth as the penalty paid for the sins of the world. As sinners under the judgment wrath of God, He took our place and paid the penalty and the price of our deliverance with His own blood. Listen to the drops of blood as they fall from hands and feet and wounded side! They voice the words, "The ransom price for my sins and for the sins of the whole world." Would that men everywhere would believe it and receive it. How dear, how precious is He to us, washed clean in His blood and freed forever from the punishment due us. *Lord, may our ransomed souls well up in praise to Thy glorious Name! Amen.*

ONE SON, HIS WELLBELOVED

*"Having yet therefore one son, his wellbeloved,
he sent him also last unto them, saying,
They will reverence my son."*
Mark 12:6

The Savior is in Jerusalem. The chief priests and scribes come to Him and question His authority. Jesus answers them in the parable of the vineyard, picturing to them the treatment of the servants who were sent to gather the fruit, telling the story—so old, so strange—of the attitude of the human heart toward God. He sent His Son, His WELLBELOVED SON, and they took

Him and killed Him and cast Him out. How could they? They have cast Him out of the schools and many of the churches, though all we have of earthly civilization and comforts today we owe to Him. *God's Wellbeloved Son, we enthrone Thee today in our hearts. Help us to worship and adore Thee. Amen.*

CHRIST, THE SON OF THE BLESSED

"Art thou the Christ, the Son of the Blessed?"
Mark 14:61

The court is convened. The High Priest is presiding. Charges had been brought against the Lord Jesus Christ by false witnesses but they had not agreed. The High Priest put to Him a question, "Art Thou the CHRIST, THE SON OF THE BLESSED?" And He answered, "I am." There was no denial of the title, but a straight confession of His Sonship, Heirship, Power and coming Glory. And when He comes—if He tarry yet a season—we will be among those who will be caught up in the clouds to meet Him in the air and with the hosts of Heaven acclaim Him "Blessed!" *Lord, Jesus Christ, Thou Son of the Blessed, hasten the glad day. Amen.*

THE KING OF THE JEWS

"And Pilate asked him, Art thou the King of the Jews? And he answering said unto him, Thou sayest it."
Mark 15:2

What a title for our Lord to put His seal upon at the time when the Jews were in subjection to the

Romans and He Himself a prisoner before a judge. But He is KING OF THE JEWS—yes, King of kings and Lord of all. Pilate will yet stand before Him to be judged, and the Jewish people will yet proclaim Him as their own King. He is the Ruler. Let us give Him His rightful place as Ruler in our lives. How can we serve Him today? Perhaps in some definite prayer for the Jewish people and some testimony to them of the joy there is in knowing, loving and serving Him. *Lord, remember Thine ancient people and all who seek to make Thee known to them. Amen.*

THE SON OF THE HIGHEST

"He shall be great and shall be called the Son of the Highest."
Luke 1:32

This is the message of the angel to Mary and here is a remarkable coincidence. In Mark 5:7, we have the evil spirit in the man in the tombs giving a similar title to Jesus, "Son of the Most High God." The title here given Him, is in fulfillment of Psalm 132:11: "The Lord hath sworn in truth unto David; he will not turn from it; of the fruit of thy body will I set upon thy throne." David's heir is to reign as Son of the Most High God, and that time only waits for the completion of the church which is His Body. Let us do our best each day to win souls for Him and thus hasten the day when we shall be with Him and reign with Him. *Son of the Highest, we bow to Thee, we worship Thee. Help us to magnify Thy name today. Amen.*

GOD MY SAVIOR

"And my spirit hath rejoiced in God my Saviour."
Luke 1:47

The word "Savior" here is "Soter" meaning "presence." Should we not imitate Mary, the blessed woman, in magnifying our Savior and rejoicing in the finished work which He hath wrought in our behalf? It is never what we are but what He is. Our joy is in Him and we rejoice with joy unspeakable and full of glory as we face this day with joyful hearts. Shall we not have a tender heart for those who do not know Him? *Savior, like a shepherd lead us today to glorify Thy name in our efforts to win souls for Thee. Amen.*

THE DAYSPRING FROM ON HIGH

"Through the tender mercy of our God;
whereby the dayspring from on high hath visited us."
Luke 1:78

Zacharias is inspired as his soul goes forth to speak of the coming of the Messiah. It has been suggested that the glory of the sunshine was breaking over the hills surrounding Jerusalem and the golden glory lighted up the horizon as his lips breathed the words inspired by the Spirit of God, "DAYSPRING FROM ON HIGH!" Perhaps the morning glory brought to the mind of Zacharias the message of Isaiah, "Arise, shine, for thy light is come and the glory of the Lord is risen upon thee." *Before we take up our daily tasks, let us turn our eyes to the heavens with grateful hearts and let the Holy Spirit flood our souls with the glory of the Risen, Coming Christ. Amen.*

HORN OF SALVATION

*"And hath raised up a horn of salvation for us
in the house of his servant David."*
Luke 1:69

Here is a title which suggests the strength and power of our Lord—"HORN OF SALVATION." The word "horn" as used in the Scripture signifies "strength" and is often found in Hebrew literature. In the horns, the bull manifests his strength. The Lord Jesus Christ is our Strength and a very present help in time of trouble (Psalms 118:14; 92:10; 28:7; 37:39). "But the salvation of the righteous is of the Lord; He is their strength in the time of trouble." You may be tempted and tried today. You may have burdens to bear. Let Him be your "HORN OF SALVATION." *Lord, strengthen us by the power of Thy might for today's service for Thee. Amen.*

THE HIGHEST

*"And thou, child,
shalt be called the
prophet of the Highest."*
Luke 1:76

Listen to the voice of Zacharias, father of John the Baptist, as he voices the wonderful prophecy concerning his son who was to be the prophet of the Lord to prepare the way before Him. Our Lord is here named "THE HIGHEST," or, better, "the Most High." He came from the heights of glory to be born in a manger. "Prophet" in the New Testament means "a public expounder" and to us,

His redeemed ones, has been committed this honorable title. We are the expounders of this great revelation of the Bible concerning our most highly exalted LORD. *Glory to God in the Highest, King of kings and Lord of lords, whom we claim as our own. Amen.*

THE BABE

"Ye shall find the babe
wrapped in swaddling clothes,
lying in a manger."
Luke 2:12

Again the voice of the angel rings out to the shepherds: "Christ the Lord—THE BABE—lying in a manger." How easy it would be for the shepherds to find Him. No other newly born babe would be found "lying in a manger"—just One—and He, the altogether lovely One, the chiefest among ten thousand! Sometimes the saints magnify their human birthright and place of birth, but He was to be a blessing to the humblest. Would not the cattle—could they have sensed the significance of the event—have bent their knees in homage to THE BABE? How sad to know that millions in our land have not yet bowed the knee to Him. *Lord, may we who have named Thy name, bow in humblest submission to Thee today and pour out our hearts in joyful praise to Thee, Thou Babe of Bethlehem. Amen.*

THE WORD

"In the beginning was the Word,
and the Word was with God,
and the Word was God."
John 1:1

W e come today to John's Gospel in which we shall
find many titles for the Son of God. Here we con-
front the first—"THE WORD." The book of Genesis commences with creation, but John commences with the
Creator. Back of all things with which we ever have had
or will have to do is *the Word.* "THE WORD was God!"
What a foundation for our faith when we know that Jesus
was the Word and the Word was God. Every day we can,
if we will, be facing this tremendous fact, and as we feel
the throb of our heart, there is a voice which says,
"God!" As we look upon the heavens and the clouds—
"God!" The sun, the moon, the trees, the flowers, the living creatures, all are saying, "God!" Without Him—
nothing! With Him—all things! *Oh, Thou Living Word,*
who hast given us the written Word, help us to abide in
Thee today. Amen.

CHRIST, THE LORD

"For unto you is born this day
in the city of David a Saviour,
which is Christ the Lord."
Luke 2:11

T he heavens are opened now and the message of the
angel of the Lord is announced—"good tidings of

great joy." The message was to the humble shepherds and it will mean much to us if we can, in humility of heart, take our place with the shepherds, acknowledge our unworthiness and appropriate the truth to our own souls—"Unto you is born a Saviour, which is CHRIST THE LORD" (the Anointed One—the Ruler). We are no longer to rule ourselves. He is to rule us. *Lord with joy we submit our wills, and surrender all to Thee. Help us to magnify Thee this day. Amen.*

THE CONSOLATION OF ISRAEL

"There was a man in Jerusalem,
whose name was Simeon;
and the same man was just and devout,
waiting for the consolation of Israel."
Luke 2:25

Simeon was just and devout and waited for the "CONSOLATION OF ISRAEL." "Consolation" means "paraclete" (One coming alongside) as we think and speak of the Holy Spirit who comes to abide in and lead us out in our daily life. Simeon was waiting for the deliverance of the Jews by the coming of the Messiah. They did not as a nation receive Him, but some did and were consoled, and Israel shall yet have the promised consolation, as Paul was comforted by the power of the indwelling Holy Spirit (1 Thessalonians 1:5). *Lord, may we also rely upon the abiding comfort of the indwelling of the Holy Spirit all the day. Amen.*

THE LORD'S CHRIST

*"And it was revealed unto him by the Holy Ghost,
that he should not see death,
before he had seen the Lord's Christ."*
Luke 2:26

Simeon was a just and devout man who believed the Word of God and rested upon its promises. The Holy Ghost came upon him and made a revelation to him. He was not to taste of death until he had tasted the sweets of seeing and knowing "THE LORD'S CHRIST." The Lord never fails His loved ones. When He can get hold of the hearts of men and women He is glad to make a revelation of Himself to them and give unto them the power of the Holy Spirit. His great heart beats in sympathy with every pulsing of every loyal-hearted follower. *Holy Spirit, give us new spiritual visions of* THE LORD'S CHRIST. *Amen.*

THE SALVATION OF GOD

"For mine eyes have seen thy salvation."
Luke 2:30

The aged saint Simeon, standing in the temple, took the child Jesus in his arms and, looking into His face, lifted his eyes to Heaven and said: "Lord, now lettest thou thy servant depart in peace, according to thy word; for *mine eyes have seen thy salvation.*" Long had he waited, long had he prayed, long had he desired to see Him. Now the Spirit of God reveals unto him the fact that his heart's desire had been granted and that he was gazing upon the Divine Savior of souls and death had no more terrors for him. There is but one cure for the world's unrest, "THE SALVATION OF GOD." Let us go out today and tell the story wherever we can. The poor, hungry-hearted, sin-sick souls are waiting. *Lord, guide us in this service to Thy Glory. Amen.*

A LIGHT TO LIGHTEN THE GENTILES

"A light to lighten the Gentiles,
and the glory of thy people, Israel."
Luke 2:32

The world has been a dark world ever since Adam and Eve listened to the temptation of Satan. There was no hope until God said: "The seed of the woman shall bruise the serpent's head"—a promise of coming victory for a lost race. He who is the light of the Gentiles is the light of the world (Matthew 4:16). The light shone for Israel first, but Israel rejected its blessed beams. But again the Light shall shine for the people now wandering over the earth in darkness. What is the duty of believers? Is it not to lift the Light high so that the world of sinners in darkness may come into fellowship with Him? *Lord of Light, help us to shine as lights in a dark world, this day. Amen.*

THE GLORY OF THY PEOPLE ISRAEL

"A light to lighten the Gentiles,
and the glory of thy people Israel."
Luke 2:32

The message of Paul was "to the Jew first," but here the Gentiles are mentioned first. The Jews turned away from Jesus and would not have Him to rule over them, but the Gentiles will not receive Him either—just a few. The glory shall rest upon Israel when He comes with sceptre in hand to rule a reconstructed earth. The Shekinah glory, manifested in the tabernacle and temple, will shine again upon His beloved people and Jesus—the Jew—will be the glory of Israel in that day. Let us love the Jews and seek to bring the Gospel of the grace of God to them. *Lord Jesus, who art* THE GLORY OF THY PEOPLE ISRAEL, *remember Thy persecuted, penalty-paying people and help us to love them. Amen.*

A SIGN

*"This child is set. . .
for a sign which shall be spoken against."*
Luke 2:34

Our Lord Jesus Christ was a significant sign to Israel. The prophecies had long before made clear that Israel was to be tested when the Messiah came. Some would believe and follow Him. Some would reject and crucify Him. Our Lord gave testimony to this fact when Pilate asked Him, "Art Thou a King?" And His answer was: "To this end was I born and for this cause came I into the world." Poor Pilate, he had his evidence but would not accept it. Where is he? THE SIGN has been given to our land, also. Where are the multitudes? The same old story will be told again and again. *Oh, Lord have compassion upon this poor land. Inspire thy servants to be brave and true in sounding the alarm. Amen.*

THE CHILD JESUS

"The child Jesus tarried behind in Jerusalem."
Luke 2:43

Here we have our first view of Jesus as a young lad, interested in the business of His Heavenly Father. Hear Him when Joseph and Mary seek Him: "Wist ye not that I must be about my Father's business?" The strangeness of the story of His life is a constant surprise. God manifested in the flesh—a Child—with words of wisdom falling from His lips—a message for us all, "Occupy (do business) till I come." Every disciple is a business man or woman, and our business is the most important in all the world. Let us take as a motto for our daily life the words of THE CHILD JESUS, "I must be about my Father's business." *Lord, help us to be busy about Thy business this day. Amen.*

Also available from

Barbour Publishing

Looking for a quick spiritual boost?
Try the 365 One-Minute Meditations series,
drawn from bestselling books and authors.

Daily Wisdom for Women
978-1-60260-371-4

Helen Steiner Rice
978-1-60260-368-4

Morning by Morning
978-1-60260-369-1

*Wonderful Names of
Our Wonderful Lord*
978-1-60260-370-7

Available wherever books are sold.